VISITOR CENTER

GEOFF GREEN

NEW YEAR'S EVE, 1996.
A time for joy and celebration, especially for those lucky enough to be spending their holidays in Yosemite Valley. Fresh snow blanketed the Sierra Nevada that day, softening the granite faces of El Capitan and Half Dome. Tents, cabins, and hotel rooms glowed with candlelight and cheer while a puzzlingly warm rain kissed 1996 good-bye.

YOSEMITE

THE 100 YEAR FLOOD

(January 1-5, 1997)

Movement in Tides

• • •

featuring

WHERE NATURE PREVAILS

by

MARK GOODIN

SIERRA PRESS
Mariposa, CA

Upper Yosemite Fall, January 2.   GLENN CROSBY

Front Cover: Half Dome and Cooks Meadow,
           January 3, 1997. (Glenn Crosby)
Frontispiece: Yosemite Valley Visitor Center,
           dusk, December 31, 1996. (Geoff Green)
Title Page: "Relocated" tent and Half Dome. (Rich
           Seiling-NPS)
Back Cover: The jumble of employee housing in
           Camp 6. (Keith Walklet-YCS)

SIERRA PRESS

ISBN 0-939365-68-5

Copyright 1997 by:
Sierra Press
4988 Gold Leaf Drive
Mariposa, CA 95338

Produced by Sierra Press for Yosemite Concession
Services, Inc.

Sierra Press is an imprint of Tellurian Press, Inc.
All rights reserved. No part of this book may be
reproduced in any form without written permission from
the publisher, except by a reviewer who may quote brief
passages of reprint a photograph.
Printed in China.
First printing, Summer 1997.
Second printing, Spring 1999.

PRODUCTION CREDITS
Book Design: Laura Bucknall and Jeff Nicholas
Editor: Nicky Leach
Photo Editor: Jeff Nicholas and Laura Bucknall
Printing coordination: Everbest Printing Co., Ltd.

ACKNOWLEDGMENTS
The publishers would like to take this opportunity
to thank the following individuals for their
assistance in the production of this book: Valerie
Trenter, Keith Walklet, and Mary Vocelka of
Yosemite Concession Services; Barbara Beroza,
Norma Craig, Dave Forgang, and Kendell
Thompson of the National Park Service; Sterling
Johnson for providing access to his video
interviews; Ron and Carol Iudice and KC Boggs of
Photo Express for their invaluable assistance; Rich
Seiling of The Ansel Adams Gallery for producing a
beautiful set of black and white prints; and finally—
a special thanks to all the photographers who made
their imagery available for review during the
editing of this title—Thank You All!

If you would like to receive a complimentary
catalog of Sierra Press publications,
please call: **(800) 745-2631**
e-mail: siepress@yosemite.net
or write: **SIERRA PRESS**
4988 Gold Leaf Drive, Mariposa, CA 95338

Upper Yosemite Fall following the New Year's Flood.

"As a geological event, these floods are not abnormal. They are a regular thing. It is the way the Earth sculpts itself. If there is a problem, it's that society, as a whole, is obsessed with a static view of the Earth. We plan for a static era. Then we're surprised when it goes through a period of rebuilding. To a river, and a watershed, life is like that of a soldier: it's 99 percent boredom and one percent terror."

Jeffrey Mount
Geology Department Chairman
University of California, Davis

"The Valley has been cleansed."

Julia Parker
Indian Cultural Demonstrator
Yosemite National Park

Morning fog in Cooks Meadow, January 3.

Debris on Superintendents Bridge, January 4.

*S*IERRA WINTER STORMS *are likely to be remembered more by the bridges and houses they carry away than by their beauty or the thousands of blessings they bring to the fields and gardens of Nature.*

John Muir
"The Mountains of California," 1894

WHERE NATURE PREVAILS

Village Store parking lot flooded by Lehamite (Indian) Creek, January 2.

AS 1996 CAME TO A CLOSE, the north-south trending peaks of California's Sierra Nevada lay hidden under a 20-foot winter snowpack—a frozen sea held in check only by winter's icy grip. The first hours of 1997 blew in on the tropical winds of a storm system that stretched far across the Pacific. As it collided with California's mountainous spine, the storm let its watery burden fall to earth. The result was a 100-Year Flood, which inundated most of central California.

A heavy snowpack followed by warm rain is not unknown, but, somehow, the threat of this kind of one-two punch occurring had either been forgotten or had fallen on deaf ears. It doesn't matter. What matters is the story of the land and the people—and the great flood that brought rejuvenation and terror.

Setting the stage for California's New Year's Flood was a winter of record-breaking rain and snow, which saturated the soil and filled reservoirs to the brim. The first day of the new year dawned with rain falling and the thermometer at a balmy 50 degrees. Park visitors, employees, and residents scanned the morning sky for a gleam of sun; finding none, they hoped things would improve as the day sobered up. But the rain continued to fall. As night fell on the first day of the year, Route 140 was closed and floodwaters isolated Yosemite Lodge. People began to feel a sense of foreboding, as they wondered what the warm rains were doing to the snowpack of Yosemite's backcountry.

By the next day, January 2, all three highways into the park were closed. Emergency crews prepared for the worst. The Merced River and the streams that feed it kept on rising. The vertical granite walls of Yosemite Valley blocked what sounds the amassing waves of snowmelt must have made as they rushed toward the valley's glacier-formed bathtub rim. By nightfall, Bridalveil, Nevada, Vernal, and Yosemite Falls were roaring forth with a god-like vengeance; their angry waters shook the air and filled the valley with a roiling mist.

Lehamite (Indian) Creek in full-flood at Yosemite Medical Clinic, January 2.

"I realized that there were some places in the park that were actually dangerous, that we shouldn't be there. It was time for us to step back, let Nature take its course, and later we'll go and look at what happened."

Steve Thompson
Wildlife Biologist, Yosemite National Park

"Indian Creek got a little high. It's supposed to go under the bridge, not around it... It just kept on getting deeper. The really big burst came later; a miniature tsunami came through the garage. You could see it coming."

Drew Leighton
Garage Custodian, Yosemite Concession Services

Emergency incident meeting, January 2.

STEVE THOMPSON - NPS

"The severity of the incident didn't sink in until the incident meeting at 2 p.m. At that point, they told us it had been raining up to an elevation of nine or ten thousand feet, and that's when we realized conditions were identical to the 1955 flood and we were probably in for a real gullywasher."

Steve Thompson
Wildlife Biologist
Yosemite National Park

The El Capitan moraine, a berm of rock and gravel left by receding glaciers, crosses the western end of the valley. The moraine slowed the floodwaters, causing them to rise and trap more than 900 park visitors and 1,200 employees on three shrinking islands. Downstream along the Merced River, hundreds of other park employees and their families in El Portal (Yosemite's gateway community and the park's administrative site) woke to find themselves unable to escape. Above and below the town, the river had bitten, chewed, and swallowed the less stable sections of Highway 140, all the way from asphalt to bedrock.

What happened during the night of January 2 almost no one saw. The curious and the adventurous who greeted the dawning of the year's third day gazed upon a serene lake where once the gentle Merced River had flowed across the valley floor. They saw bridges, roads, building, campgrounds, tents, cars, and trucks ravaged and destroyed.

Thousands of people were trapped in Yosemite Valley, threatened by a potential shortage of clean drinking water and the fear of disease and infection from the sewage-contaminated floodwaters. Bolstered by the news that the American Red Cross, the State Office of Emergency Services, the Mariposa County Sheriff's Department, the Highway Patrol, and even the military were coming to the rescue, most of the afflicted took a window seat and watched as a once-in-a-lifetime event took place: the awakening of the Merced River.

As the flood slowly waned, emergency workers prepared to evacuate the valley. Airlifting people out by Chinook helicopter was considered but determined too hazardous. Finally, in the twilight hours of January 3, all the visitors and some employees were escorted out in their own vehicles along Highway 41 to Fish Camp and safety. It would take ten weeks and $10 million before Yosemite Valley could welcome visitors again.

Few remember Yosemite looking more alive than it does today, so free of the hand of man. The antediluvian banks of the Merced River were nearly empty of natural debris, long picked clean or packed smooth by humans. The river now holds a jumble of logs and limbs, a tumble of brush and rocks, providing habitat for plants, fish, amphibians, birds, and mammals.

Water and floods cannot damage Yosemite's natural environment—they are a part of it; they are its lifeblood.

Entrance to Lower River Campground, January 2.

The flood destroyed half of Yosemite Valley's 900 campsites. Hundreds of picnic tables, bear-proof food storage boxes, waste cans, and fire grates were washed down the river. The Lower River, Upper River, and Lower Pines campgrounds will be rebuilt out of the floodplain at an estimated cost of $3 million.

Merced River, El Portal, January 2.

Merced River at Park entrance, Highway 140, January 2.

"...what you really notice is the sound of thunder—from beneath the river, as huge boulders smash into each other, as if the gods are bowling; you can even see sparks fly occasionally—underwater!"

Jerry Rankin
Editor
Mariposa Gazette

"If the water had been able to go under the bridge, it wouldn't have happened. There were trees sandwiched with 20x40 foot chunks of asphalt up against the bridge. The water just came around the flood wall... I'll get over it some year. You walk around some days; you think you are in control, but you are not. Everything has suddenly changed."

Letty Barry
Owner—Yosemite Redbud Lodge and
Sisochi Gallery at Savage's Trading Post

Opposite: Yosemite Redbud Lodge and Savage's Trading Post, evening of January 2 and morning of January 3.

Yosemite Chapel, January 3.

"Why is the park here? It is to let natural processes prevail.
This certainly was a big natural process."
Steve Thompson
Wildlife Biologist, Yosemite National Park

Broken sewer line, Cookie Cliff, January 3.
JOHN REYNOLDS

The 7.5 miles of Highway 140 between Yosemite and El Portal received heavy damage, with 19 sections completely destroyed. One section of the highway, known as "Cookie Cliff," was washed away leaving a hole in the road 300 feet long and taking the main sewer line for the Park with it.

South Fork, Merced River, Wawona, January 2.
CHRISTINE LOBERG

"It won't get much higher,
or there won't be anything left."
Al Gordon
Author/Historian

"The other deputies and I got rashes from
being in the water. We were right downstream
from the [wastewater] treatment plant. . . We
were in the water for quite awhile. We didn't
have anything to change into; we stayed in our
wet, contaminated clothes into the next day. I
think our exposure was kind of extended."
Deputy Kathy Rumfelt
Mariposa County Sheriff's Department

I WAS STARTLED by a sudden thundering crash. . . This was the flood wave of Yosemite Creek. . . with volume tenfold increased beyond its spring-time fullness, it took its place as leader of the glorious choir.

• • •

THE MOUNTAIN waters, suddenly liberated, seemed to be holding a grand jubilee ...the whole Valley throbbed and trembled, and was filled with an awful, massive, solemn, sea-like roar.

John Muir
"The Yosemite," 1912

Yosemite Creek, January 2.

Yosemite Valley drains an area of 217,131 mountainous acres. During the flood's peak, the gauging station at Pohono Bridge, in Yosemite Valley's western end, measured the river's flow at 24,600 cubic feet per second. During the four peak hours of the flood, more than a billion tons of water poured into the Valley. The force of the water, as it hurtled down the 2,000-foot drop in elevation between the Valley and El Portal, created 20-foot tall standing waves in the Merced River.

JOHN REYNOLDS (BOTH)

*"Yosemite Falls was thundering so loud that
our windows were shaking in the house, and
we were a half mile away from the waterfall.
It was just roaring!"*

Sue Beatty
Documentary Photographer

*"Rangers told me it was uncanny the way
the Valley filled up with water. In certain
areas, that water raced along causing great
damage, but in others it was a gentle lake."*

Karl Kroeber
The Yosemite Fund

THE FLOOD reached its peak late on the night of January 2, its most spectacular and violent moments shrouded in darkness. When the sun rose on January 3, the worst was over. The people of Yosemite and El Portal were alternately filled with awe and grief. Tomorrow they would begin their journey down the long road to recovery.

The effort to rebuild Yosemite may cost as much as $178 million; a third of that money will be spent removing park buildings and infrastructure from the floodplain. The recovery cost is a sound investment, however, when considering the economic impact of a fully functioning Yosemite National Park. One recent analysis determined that the 4.1 million annual visitors to the park provide $2.1 billion in economic benefits each year.

For many of the people who worked for Yosemite Concession Services (the company operating most of the food service, lodging, and retail operations in the park) the flood brought heartbreak and loss. Quarters for 468 employees were flooded under six feet of water or more. One hundred sixty canvas cabins floated completely off their foundations (80 at Ozone and 80 at Camp 6.) Hundreds of people who worked and lived in the park for years—people who called Yosemite home—were left unemployed and homeless.

Campground damaged by flood waters, January 4.

KEITH WALKLET-YCS

"By the time I boxed my stuff up, the water was up to my knees. I slept on the floor of the cafeteria with about 150 other employees and guests."

Stan Wacht
Food Service
Yosemite Concession Services

"I never got back to my room until it was all over with. The water line was five feet high—it was too late."

Drew Leighton
Garage Custodian
Yosemite Concession Services

Displaced employee housing, January 3.

Employee housing in Camp 6, January 3.

"The tent cabin where I lived was smashed up against a telephone pole 30 feet downstream. I'm still cleaning up two and a half months later."

Brent Benson
Food Service
Yosemite Concession Services

Buckled asphalt near Happy Isles. Inset: Pohono Bridge damage, January 3.

All highways into Yosemite Valley, as well as nine road bridges inside the Park, were damaged by the flood waters. The estimated cost to repair them: $36 million. The flood also washed away parts of ten archeological sites in the Valley—two with known human remains. In addition, at least five historic dumps were exposed, causing potential health and safety hazards as well as creating a temptation for looters.

GEOFF GREEN, INSET: GEOFF GREEN

Thirty-three trail bridges throughout the Park are known to have been destroyed or severely damaged and much of the 800-mile trail system was damaged by erosion. Repairing the damage will cost approximately $4 million.

Highway 140, washed out in El Portal, January 3.

JEFF NICHOLAS

"Everyone was saying I couldn't get home because of the water. The rangers wouldn't let me through, but I told them I had two daughters at home and I had to get there. So they radioed ahead and I made it through. We were together, which made me feel safe, even though I knew everything was crazy everywhere else."

Charity Kirkpatrick
Cashier, Yosemite Concession Services

"It's important to realize that what happened here is supposed to happen. It's part of the Valley, it's not something that was an aberration. It's not something you can count on not happening again— because it's going to."

Geoff Green, Naturalist
Yosemite National Park

Emergency personnel and equipment, Ahwahnee Meadow, January 3. Inset: Emergency medical evacuation in progress.

"It was a nightmare. It was like every time you did one thing, something else blew up... and then it snowed eight inches."

Alan Palisca
Maintenance Mechanic
Yosemite National Park

New Year's visitors finally able to leave Yosemite Valley, January 3. Inset: Truck flipped by force of raging water.

"It was just so overwhelming. It's amazing how small we are compared to the forces of nature."
Trish Hall-Jones
Volunteer, American Red Cross

"Our truck was the only one that flipped. I saw it a lot on TV, still do. A color picture of it is even on the Internet."
Jerry Conley Sr.
Conley Construction, Oakhurst, CA

Flooding in Foresta, January 2.

"The windows in Residence One [the old Superintendent's residence, now used for offices] were rattling; the walls were rattling from the force of Yosemite Falls. That was a constant reminder that this was really an extreme event."

Steve Thompson
Wildlife Biologist
Yosemite National Park

"I guess the perspective you get about it is that essentially this is the course that Nature takes—and it's going to occur again and again and again, and the only real difference between now and 100,000 years ago is the presence of human beings and their structures—and they kind of get in the way.

Leroy Radanovich
Photographer/Historian

Engine compartment of Yosemite Valley Tram, January 5.

"All these vehicles were under nine to ten feet of water. It was a mountain of work. . . It was really depressing to see our babies so hammered."

Ron Silva
Mechanic
Yosemite Concession Services

Reflection of Half Dome in window of Residence One (note waterline on window). Inset: Interior of employee housing after flood.

"It was a spiritual experience that will never leave me."

Jay Johnson

Forestry Foreman, Yosemite National Park

"People just weren't ready for this."

Stan Wacht, Food Service

Yosemite Concession Services

Flood damage, Yosemite Lodge. Inset: Back wall of Parkline Restaurant, El Portal.

KEITH WALKLET - YCS, INSET: JOE MOLHOEK - NPS

Because of the flood, nearly one-quarter of the lodging in the Park will not be available for use by the public in 1997. This will affect the vacation plans of more than 200,000 visitors. At Yosemite Lodge, 189 cabins and 108 motel rooms were flooded to depths of five feet and more. The historic Ahwahnee and Wawona Hotels rode through the flood unscathed.

Freshly deposited sand, Merced River below El Portal, January 3.

"We now have a beach for a backyard, where grass and rocks had been before. Our neighbor's picnic table is up in a tree behind our house."

Dawn, 17-year-old student
Yosemite Park High School

"All my old favorite swimming holes are gone, but I guess that means there are a lot of new ones to explore and enjoy now."

Eamon Schneider
20-year-old native of El Portal

El Capitan from near Bridalveil Fall, January 4.

GEOFF GREEN

"Being Native American, and from here [Yosemite], I know our people have always had really close ties to the Valley—in a spiritual sense. Our grandfather made a statement: when the last of our people leaves Yosemite Valley the rocks are going to start coming down."

Jay Johnson
Forestry Foreman
Yosemite National Park

YOSEMITE VALLEY AND the mountains that cradle it are a work in progress. First impressions of the New Year's Flood of 1997 paint the event as a major rite of passage in the life of the valley. Half Dome's mute stone would surely say: "You should have been here a million years ago." Yosemite's oldest residents, the giant sequoias—some 2,000 years old or more—have seen twenty such "100-year-floods" in their lifetimes.

The unusually large and early snowpack that covered the High Sierra and Yosemite was not unheard of, nor was the type of warm storm that followed, known affectionately as a "Pineapple Express." It is the combination of the two that is rare. Similar storms of lesser magnitude occurred in 1867, 1871, 1937, 1950, and 1955. What remains to be seen is whether such floods are occurring more frequently, and if so, why?

The Merced River: shaper, nurturer, comforter, destroyer. It seemed the true ruler of Yosemite during those first three days of 1997, and as the waters abated, few dissenting opinions were heard. At its height, the people of El Portal could feel the ground tremble from boulders rolling along the river bottom a quarter mile away. The New Year's Flood stripped the banks of the Merced River bare, cracked and smashed granite boulders, eroded cliffs, and cut bedrock. This is how the river canyon grew to its present size and how it will continue to grow.

Emergency repairs, salvage operations, and long-term planning for park restoration efforts are underway and will continue for another four or five years. Guiding the recovery effort is Yosemite's General Management Plan (GMP), a National Park Service document completed in 1980 after a long period of public review. The

Opposite: Road damage below Cookie Cliff, January 3. Inset: Road crew beginning repairs below Cookie Cliff.

Black bear tracks in fresh snow, January 5.

"This is still a wild place."
Drew Leighton
Garage Custodian
Yosemite Concession Services

primary goals of the GMP are to reduce cars and congestion, reclaim priceless natural beauty, and allow natural processes to prevail. These goals guide the rebuilding of Yosemite.

The hardest hit of the flood's victims were the employees of Yosemite Concession Services, mostly basic wage earners with no insurance. More than 1,000 employees were laid off during the closure of the park. Only 70% of them have been able to return to their jobs. Others wait; some will never come back.

The storm's impact on Yosemite's high country is still unknown. Immediately after the flood, another winter storm blanketed the region with snow, preventing the National Park Service from assessing the damage to the hundreds of miles of trails and dozens of footbridges in the high country. As this book went to press, many questions remained unanswered.

For the natural world—the world that needs no guidance or help from man—this flood was no disaster; it was a birthday, a wiping clean of the slate, a day in the life of the earth. We humans have difficulty appreciating such a long-term view. When acts of nature, or God, or—worse yet—man tear apart our homes, our livelihoods, and the very earth around us, then the pace of change becomes too swift for us. For nature, the flood brought promises of new life. For many of those who live here, it was a tragedy measured in tears, exhaustion, and great personal loss. For most, during the event, it was a tremendous physical and emotional drain. All shared a sense of awe at what they had lived through. Amazingly, not a single human life was taken by the flood.

The river is quiet now; new growth already shades much of the clean, scraped granite. The memory of those first few days of 1997 fades from the land, but not from the lives, hearts, and minds of the people of Yosemite, El Portal, and the upper Merced. They will never forget the sights and sounds of their world changing overnight.

Great blue heron in Merced River, January 5.

"I feel privileged to have been here and seen an event like this."

Steve Thompson
Wildlife Biologist
National Park Service

Upper Yosemite Fall, January 3.

JOHN REYNOLDS

Y

OSEMITE VALLEY IS AS BEAUTIFUL AS EVER.

Events such as this most recent flood helped create the spectacular natural beauty of Yosemite, and essentially the natural environment remains little changed.

The natural environment of the park is adapted for periodic flooding. The structures and the infrastructure we have built in the park are not so well adapted.

The flooding provided us with a field test to confirm the wisdom of the plans for the future of Yosemite, as well as an opportunity to accelerate the implementation of the General Management Plan and restore part of the Valley. We now have a chance to make long-called-for and widely supported changes in Yosemite. Nature has already begun a process that people have only talked about. As we build, we want to avoid the mistakes of the past.

It's abundantly clear that natural processes should not be ignored.

B.J. Griffin
Superintendent
Yosemite National Park